ACROSTIC MOTIVATIONS

A POETIC COLLECTION

DR. SONIA GUPTA

DEDICATED TO
MY DEAR FATHER

YOU CAN NOT BE REPLACED

You are my king; my role model,
O' you hold my hands in every odd and hurdle,
Under the umbrella of your love, I always lived joyfully,

Can't forget what you have done for me,
Always guided me to follow the right path,
Never let me fall down even in the dark,

Nourished me with nutrients of love and care,
O' dad, you never left me wild and bare,
Taught valuable teachings of life,

Became a pillar to stand in every strife,
Enlightened a candle of selfless love,

Rare treasure you are, God had sent from above,
Epitome of sacrifices, devotion, and principles,
Painted my life with lovable colours,
Leaving this materialistic world, you have gone away,
And even then, with me, you always stay,
Can feel your presence always with us,
Everything can be replaced in the world,
Dear dad to replace you is totally impossible.

Contents

Contents

Contents

Foreword

MAGNIFICIENT COLLECTION IN A UNIQUE STYLE

To inspire human beings through fascinating, attractive, and informative style in a simple way has always been the first goal of poetry. *Acrostic Motivations* is a magnificent collection of 50 motivational poems written in the Acrostic genre by the poetess Dr. Sonia Gupta. She has authored eleven independent books, out of which eight are in English and three are in the Hindi language. This is her ninth independent English poetry book.

An acrostic poem is a poem where certain letters in each line spell out a word or phrase. Mostly, the first letters of each line are used to spell the message. This form of poetry is very interesting and challenging. Accepting the challenge of this special poetic style, Dr. Sonia has composed many exquisite poems. The main theme of these poems is motivation and inspiration. Reading this style not only makes the poetry interesting but also inspires readers to capture the message behind the written verses.

Literature reveals that acrostic form has various subtypes like conventional, double, abecedarian, mesostich, telestich, and golden shovel. Here in this collection, the poetess has used the conventional style, where the poem is composed beginning with the first letter of the words included in the poem's title.

This style of Acrostic form can be well appreciated in the beginning of this collection itself where the poetess has dedicated her work to her late father by composing the poem "You cannot be replaced" in Acrostic style which makes the collection very unique and special. The importance of the Father has been well explained in this poem. The last line of the poem is extremely important, where twenty-four carats of truth have been represented:-

"Rare treasure you are, God had sent from above,
Epitome of sacrifices, devotion, and principles,
Painted my life with lovable colors,
Leaving this materialistic word, you have gone away,
And even then, with me, you always stay,
Can feel your presence always with us,
Everything can be replaced in the world,
Dad to replace you is totally impossible"!!!

Some excerpts from the poems of this collection demonstrating the conventional style of acrostic poetry are given below:-

"Mysterious is this life and its story.
Impossible may turn into a glory.
Roses bloom even with the prickly thorns.
Aha! moon smiles even in the gloom.
Cactus survives even in hot sandy desert.
Life suddenly takes so many twists.
Enclosed by its hurdles we get tired sometimes.

Suddenly some miracles happen at that time."
(Miracles do happen in life)

"Creativity is an art.
Rejuvenate new ideas to start.
Entwine pure thoughts in mind.
Allowing you to think divine.
Thoughts that are created.
Enter the world where we live."

(Create something meaningful)

When poems inspire us, their importance in our life increases a lot. From this point of view, a poet has a lot of responsibility in writing. According to Welsh poet Dylan Thomas, "A good poem is a contribution to reality. The world is never the same once a good poem has been added to it. A good poem helps to change the shape of the universe, helps to extend everyone's knowledge of himself and the world around him." In the light of this statement, if we look at the poems in this collection ignite the inner inspiration and motivation of the readers through these verses:-

"Even if the night is too dark.
Veil of this dark beholds shimmering spark.
Even if the monsoon clouds are black.
New rays of rainbow dance in their lap."

(Even the darkness has a light)

"Believe in your dreams O' dear.

Enliven them forever and cheer.

Let these dreams be your inspiration.

Ignite within a flicker of determination.

Even if your dreams do not come true.

Victory may not always embrace you.

Even if everything seems unfair".

(Do believe in your dreams)

Few poems of the collection also reflect the vivid shades of life:-

"The moments never stop, they move on.

In every moment something is hidden.

Memories become unforgettable lessons.

Enriching life with experiences to learn."

(Memorable moments of time)

Through a few poems, the poetess has tried to motivate readers by following real facts about life. Like beauty, distance, smile, judgment, doubt, etc. This variety of content, keeping the main theme focused within the collection, makes it special:-

"Then also, wrinkled skin glows.

The harmless impact it throws."

(Even the wrinkled skin glows)

"Doubt; a five-lettered word.
O' but deep meaning it beholds.
Unnecessary obstacles in the way of life.
Biggest enemy that kills without a knife.
Throwing us into a dilemma."

(Doubt is the biggest enemy)

Imagination is the unique power owned by a poet. In a few of poems, the poetess has composed beautiful imaginary verses:-

"Wearing the wings of fantasy.
Imagine being a galaxy.
Nuclear atoms, electrons, and photons.
Glittering like silver and diamond.
Sometimes becoming a prince or princess."

(Wearing the wings of fantasy)

"The world is a play stage to play.
Humans are actors in a unique way.
Everyone plays their own role till the end.

When the play ends, the curtain is turned."

(The world is a play stage)

In brief, I would say that ACROSTIC MOTIVATION- a collection of poetry, is composed of vivid forms of inspiration and motivation reflecting both the bitter truth and joyful aspects of life. I believe that readers will surely like this collection of poems. No any doubt that Poetess Dr. Sonia's poetry will be widely read and appreciated as usual. My endless greetings to her.

- Dr. Shailesh Gupta Veer
(Poet & Reviewer)
Fatehpur, UP, India
Email: editorsgveer@gmail.com

Preface

When the very first time, I read this poem written by the famous poet "Edger Allan Poe", I found something unique and interesting in it. That raised my curiosity to learn more about this poetry. And on my research, I came to know that this was a special form of poetry known as "ACROSTIC". And I fell in love with it. Since then, I dreamed to write my own book on ACROSTIC Poems. And today, that dream has come true".

Hi dear all,

Myself, Dr. Sonia Gupta is again before you with my 9th independent English Poetry book. Before this, my all 8 poetry books were based on normal poetic verses. But this book "ACROSTIC MOTIVATIONS" is a collection of acrostic poems solely. And the main theme of these poems is motivation/ inspiration. That guided me to choose the title too.

"Poetry is the rhythmical creation of beauty in words".
(Edger Allan Poe)

Very well said by the famous poet "Edger Allan Poe"; when thoughts of the mind are flown into the ink of the poet's pen, it gives birth to poetry that enchants a rhythm adding beauty to the simple words.A poet is blessed with a magical wand by the great Almighty that has the power to turn words into art.

English literature is very deep and beholds a vivid range of poetic forms that are unique in their own. 'Acrostic' poetry is one of such forms that beholds a special style. With this form, a poet can embed hidden meanings, dwell inspiration, or simply bring fun to the readers with the unique structure of poetry.

'Acrostic' poetry is a form of poetry, wherein a certain letter in each line spells out a word or phrase. Most often, the first letters of each line are used to spell the message, but they can appear anywhere. Based on which Acrostic poems can be divided into various subtypes such as:

1. Conventional acrostic: In this, the first letter or word of each line is to spell out a related word or phrase. It is the commonest form of acrostic.

2. Double acrostic: It embeds a message both *at the beginning and at the end of each line.* The first letter of each line spells out a word, and so does the last letter of each line.

3. The abecedarian acrostic: Here, the first letter of each line runs in alphabetical order.

4. Mesostich acrostic: In which a word or phrase is formed *down the middle of the poem.*

5. Telestich: A relatively uncommon form of an acrostic. It forms words or

phrases using *the last letters of each line.*

6. Golden Shovel: Here, the last word of each line should be read vertically so that it transcribes the text of another poem.

Famous acrostic poems throughout history have used the form to write love letters, incite political rebellions, and play with form. From the abecedarian to the golden shovel, acrostic poetry hijacks the poem's use of line breaks. A detailed description of these types can be read through internet resources or related books.

My current collection is composed of 50 acrostic poems that dwell on motivational messages. All poems are of the conventional type of acrostic. I hope, all of you will enjoy reading these poems and the melody of acrostic will enchant music around you that will dwell inspiration and motivation to everyone. Although we all are already motivated, poetry is one of the commonest boosters of motivation.

Without saying much more, let me finish here with the hope that as usual, my contribution will be appreciated by everyone around.

Yours truly

Dr. Sonia Gupta

Acknowledgements

Gratitude is a single word, but deep meaning it beholds. I usually hear these words "If we say Thank you to someone, it means we are bowing our head in front of that Lord only". One can forget anything in life, but should never forget to thank someone who has helped us in any way.

First of all, I thank the Goddess of words *"Maa Saraswati"* who gave me the strength to complete this work of mine and gave shape to my simple words to paint a beautiful canvas that would be worthwhile to preserve forever in the hearts of readers.

In this world, everything changes, but one thing that never ever changes is *"our parents"*. Heartfelt thanks to my parents for their faith and showering their infinite blessings on me! Special thanks to my father who has left this materialistic world attaining the embrace of the divine Lord. He had been my inspiration forever and his teachings illuminate my life's pathway like an enlightening candle.

A Token of thanks to sir, *"Dr. Shailesh Gupta Veer"* for writing a wonderful foreword for my book. Thank you sir for all your blessings and guidance.

Teachers are the selfless builders of our life, A word of Thanks to all my respected teachers who always showed me the right path in my life and brimmed my heart with their blessings.

Lovable token of gratitude to my *brothers, sisters, and all family*members for their love and support always.

Friends are the precious ornaments gifted by God, who without any blood relation, make a bonding of forever relation. My thankful regard to all my friends far and near.

I would like to thank my students too, who always cherished my poetry in the lecture hall and kept my dream alive inside to get transformed into reality one day.

Last but not least, it will be unfair if I forget to thank the 'notion press' publication through which my book is going to be published. Thanks to, entire team for the cooperation.

Thank you, readers, fellow poets, and friends for all your love and appreciation!!!

DR. SONIA GUPTA

Biography Of Poetess

DR. SONIA GUPTA is an Oral Pathologist (BDS, MDS) from, Chandigarh in India. Though, a doctor by profession, poetry is her passion. She has been writing since 2006. She is a trilingual poetess and writes in English, Hindi, and Punjabi languages. She is a prolific writer and has written more than 3000 verses in the above languages. She has established herself as a renowned poetess after getting her eleven independent poetry books, out of which three are in Hindi and eight in English. This is her 9th independent English poetry book.

She has won many prizes in poetry and story writing competitions organized by various literary groups on Facebook and other literary platforms. She won a gold and silver medal in a poetic world cup contest held by Nigeria in Feb and May 2018 respectively. She has been awarded "PRASANNA JENN MEMORIAL AWARD 2018" by the Asian Literary Society. She got 5th rank in the International Essay writing competition on 'Skin complexion discrimination' organized by literary society, India in March 2018, One of her essays 'Our role & responsibilities towards nation was selected in a national essay writing competition and is a part of book 'Youth as nation builders; a collection of 41 essays published by lab academia.

She has been awarded several awards in Hindi literature. And her Hindi compositions are part of various anthologies, newspapers, and magazines.

Her English poems have been published in more than 50 anthologies such as " DIVINE MADNESS", "BOUQUETS OF LOVE & VERSES", "CHRISTMAS", "HUMANITY & PEACE" by Ardus Publications ; "THE REEEST VERSES" and "NIBSTEARS CAVE ANTHOLOGY FOR PEACE" by Nibstear society; "ROSES & RHYMES" by Serene publication; 'FRAGRANCE OF ASIA', 'YOU AND ME', 'INFINITY', 'EAST MET

WEST', 'PEACE LOVER', 'HEARTISTRY', 'QUEEN', 'RAINDROPS OF LOVE', 'TENUOUS BREATHS OF GIRLS' by VISHWBHARTI RESEARCH CENTER; 'HOPE REBORNE','MERI KAHANI' By Lab academia; 'WORLD BOOK OF POETS' by Sourav Sarkar; 'FRAGRANCE OF LOVE', LEAVES OF POETREE' by Writtenrock publication; 'WORLD HEALING WORLD PEACE' by Inner child press; 'BUTTERFLY LOVE', 'GIGLING PEN', 'POETIC CHRISTMAS', I AM A WOMAN', 'THE GOLDEN CROP', 'SUMMER RAIN', 'HEAT IS ON', 'THE MILLINEAL POETS', 'ONLY YOU' by poetry planet; 'VASUDHA-2' by raindrop publication; 'COMPLEXION BASED DISCRIMINITIES' by Notion press; 'GLOMAG -18' by Cyberwit publication; 'STONE AEROPLANE', 'REPUBLIC DAY', 'BONJOUR FEVRIER', 'BUTTERFLY' 'CYNDRELLA' by Spectrum publication; 'CHRISTMAS', 'In the memory of 1952' by Poetry of moon; 'PETALS OF LOVE', 'GEMS OF POESY', 'KALEIDOSCOPE OF ASIA', 'UNTAMED THRILLS & SHRILLS' by Asian literary society; 'SPRING- WINDOW TO PEACE' by Poetry for peace group, 'WORLD POETRY ON LET THERE BE PEACE' by Global feternity of poets publication; 'GATHERING WORDS' by Lanere lekan; 'VOICE OF VOICELESS' by Yes 2 publication and many more.

Her writings have been published in various newspapers and magazines. She is aregular contributor to monthly online magazines like "Hall of poets", "Reflection" and "Glomag" and international journals like "Research Inspiration", "Research imbibition" & "Jai Maa Saraswati Gyandayani". Her poetic journey continues with a great endeavor. Her poetry and writings reflect her closeness and deep love for nature, life, and spirituality. For her, poetry is a God-gifted boon and she wishes to fly high wearing the wings of poetry. Her many projects are coming soon.

Besides poetry, she is fond of paintings, singing, cooking, knitting, designing, stitching and embroidery too. She has won many awards in art competitions too. Many of her paintings have been placed on the cover pages of various anthologies. She has even designed the cover page on her own for her two English anthologies. She has got her own blog, youtube channel, Facebook page, and Instagram profile.

Dr. Sonia Gupta is also contributing to the literature of her own professional field. Her several scientific papers have been published in indexed national and international journals with the first authorship. She is also working as a reviewer of various journals. She has also written two textbooks on her subject of specialization in dentistry, which is under publication process. Presently, she is working as a faculty in a prestigious dental institute near her city. And along with her profession, she is enjoying her passion too.

CONTACT DETAILS:

ADDRESS- #95/3, Adarsh Nagar, Dera Bassi, Dist: Mohali, Punjab-140507, India.

MOBILE- 6280420736, 8054951990

FACEBOOK ID - 100004964983747@facebook.com

FACEBOOK PAGE - https://www.facebook.com/sonia4840/

BLOG - http://drsoniablogspot.blogspot.in/

E MAIL - Sonia.4840@gmail.com

YOUTUBE CHANNEL https://www.youtube.com/channel/UCKF2jM5P8VDjZ9fBZLBTRHA

INSTAGRAM ID: https://instagram.com/gdrsonia?igshid=YmMyMTA2M2Y=

ACROSTIC
MOTIVATIONS

1. MIRACLES DO HAPPEN IN LIFE

Mysterious is this life and its story
Impossible may turn into glory
Roses bloom even with the prickly thorns
Aha! moon smiles even in the gloom
Cactus survives even in the hot sandy desert
Life suddenly takes so many twists
Enclosed by its hurdles we get tired sometimes
Suddenly some miracles happen at that time

Dark clouds get impregnated with raindrops
O' drizzling on plants, trees, and crops

How a tiny seed in a mother's womb
After nine months, sprouts out to be a boon
Patients pushed towards the door of death
Perceive this life again as a rebirth
Even the bare land blooms into a garden
Newborn starts crawling on his own

Invisible air leaves an aromatic spell
Nobody knows what is the origin of a shell

Little birds start flying themselves
Involving just seven surs, melodious rhymes develop
For sure, miracles do happen to bring smiles to abound
Endless are the examples around

2. DEATH IS NOTHING BUT ANOTHER LIFE

Death is the universal truth
Everyone is afraid of it but
And the fact is that nobody of us realizes
That death is nothing, but another life
Hey, who says that we die ever?

In fact, we perceive a new birth O' dear
Soul is immortal, only the body is temporary

Never ever it dies O' buddy
Only thing is that it just changes its costumes
Throwing away old, wearing new
Happily, it opens a new door
In which a new life it explores
Nobody knows how many rebirths it takes
God's fragment it is, it never ever breaks

Beautiful is the meaning of death
Under its embrace, a new life it protects

Teaching everyone a lesson

All around, nothing is permanent
Never ever be afraid of embracing this death
O' but sow good seeds, that is the fact
The seeds as you sow, so shall you reap
Have the vision to visualize your every deed
Enlighten a candle of divinity in your heart
Rejuvenate the virtues of humanity in each part

Live your life treading the right path
Illuminating your eternal spark
For sure, you will cherish this truth
Elders say right, 'death is nothing but another birth'

3. EVERYONE HAS GOT SOME STORY

Everyone has to face the stride
Venturing the voyage of life
Everyone is enclosed with vivid hurdles
Rolling in the lap of struggle.
Yet sometimes we can't even cry
O' sometimes even tears become dry
Nobody is there to share our misery
Engulfed by the worm of agony

Heart gets dwelled with despair
At that time, everything seems unfair
Surrounded by the gloom of stress

Getting captured in cobweb of hopelessness
Often we forget even our own power
There is nothing left to enjoy and cheer

Some fight even being alone
Opting for the courage they move on

Making their own pathway
Embracing new adventurous ways

Scribbling a glittering glory
That too is masked by another story
O' a story that is written with painful words
Rocking they are today, but deeply pierced
You stop mourning, like you they are also hurt

4. CREATE SOMETHING MEANINGFUL

Creativity is an art
Rejuvenate new ideas to start
Entwine pure thoughts in mind
Allowing you to think divine
Thoughts that are created
Enter the world where we live

Sow the seeds of optimistic thoughts
O' seek to carve diamond from coal
Magical are these tiny thoughts
Either evoke or provoke
This is in your control
How to manage them as whole
Inspire yourself to discover new avenues
Never allow creativity that ruins
Generate thoughts that are meaningful

Master your mind to think beautiful
Enrich these thoughts with positivity
And give birth to purposeful creativity

ACROSTIC MOTIVATIONS

Nurture your thoughts with nutrients of love
In every thought let compassion dwell
Never allow the mind to go astray
Guide it to think in the right way
Finally, you will see
Unbelievable masterpiece
Leading towards eternal joy and peace

5. EVEN THE WRINKLED SKIN GLOWS

Eyes get old with time moving on
Veins get shrunken and torn
Ears lose the power to listen
Numb and wrinkled becomes the skin

Then also, wrinkled skin glows
The harmless impact it throws
Enriching others with abundant prosperity

Wrinkled it is, yet entangled with beauty
Roses bloom in its embrace
Innocent smile greets the face
Nobody knows the secret of this glow
Kind of a miraculous spell it throws
Letting everyone learn a lesson
Even when we get old, we are young
Do you know? what makes it so?

Smile; that keeps it aglow

Kind and empathetic heart
In which love and compassion dwell
Nurturing the mind with soulful thoughts

Giving others joy and hope
Lovable is this lesson to learn
O' beauty is not the slave of anyone
Wearing glowing garments or ornaments is not beauty
Simple living with divine thoughts is the real beauty

6. AN ACT PORTRAYED BY HEART

Away from any burden or boundaries
Nectar that can erase all worries

An act that brims heart with joy and passion
Canvas painted with vivid shades of emotions
Touches millions of souls and hearts

Portraying a masterpiece that is known as 'art'
O' art is an act that is not limited to time
Rejuvenates new ideas in the mind
The flicker of hope in hopelessness
Ray of light in the darkness
An act that is the reflection of an artist's inner self
Yielding a portrait in which lively feelings dwell
Enlightening a candle of profound mirth
Drains away all agony and dearth

Blooming like a flower in the life's garden
Yacht, that silently flows in a river of emotions

Having a magical wand that brings miracles
Encourages to do something special
Art is an act that is portrayed by the heart
Remains forever even after death departs
This is a devotion; not just any task

7. SILENCE SPEAKS MANY THINGS

Silently, the sun rises in the morning
In the veil of night, stars silently keep on dancing
Look, how the moon silently romances with its moonlight
Even being silent, so beautiful is the eventide
Nose, ear, and eyes, silently speak
Cherishing the world's beauty that is unique
Enlightening candle smiles even being silent

Silently eeds grow up into trees and plants
Pages of books silently narrate a story
Even being silent, the pen moves freely
Aha! silently breeze blows singing a melody
Kites flying high mesmerize everybody
Silently, fishes keep on buzzing amidst waves

Meadows and crops embrace muddy pathways
Aroma of flowers blooms in life's garden
No voice, yet the flowing river is serene
Yachts and ships sail in the sea quietly

Tortoises and turtles roll silently
How beautifully this silence tweets
Its style is amazing and so very unique
Not every time there is a need to speak loudly
Silence speaks many things quietly

8. YOU ARE BORN FOR A PURPOSE

You are the Great Lord's creation
O' he created you for a plan
Under his grace, you perceive this life

And you don't know where you will ride
Rare treasure is this human life
Everyone doesn't get it twice

Blessed you are to get a human birth
O' you are born for a purpose on this earth
Relieving others' pains and sufferings
Nurturing hearts with blessings

For dwelling humanity around
O' for spreading smile abound
Reviving divine energy within

And to bury all envies and sins

Purposes may be endless
Until we find the best
Real purpose is to achieve salvation
Performing good deeds in the right direction
O' life is nothing but a cycle of death and birth
Sowing seeds of good deeds we can perceive profound mirth
Embracing Lord's divine grace forever is the real purpose

9. DISTANCE DOES NOT MATTER

Distance does not matter
If there is faith and true love O' dear
Someone may be far away
To speak with them, there is no way
Alas! We can't see them
Neither we can greet them
Closed are all the windows and doors
Embarrassed we are missing our beloveds

Drowned in their memories
O' we want to meet our buddies
Entwining vivid thoughts in mind
So tough is to spend that time

No call, no talks, no message
O' but the distance doesn't matter
They are always within our hearts

Moving along even if they are apart

Accompanying us like the blowing breeze
Though being silent, they always speak
Through their eternal existence
Enrich our life with their sweet fragrance
Reminding us of their presence

10. DOUBT IS THE BIGGEST ENEMY

Doubt; a five-lettered word
O' but a deep meaning it beholds
Unnecessary obstacle in the way of life
*Become **an** enemy that kills without a knife*
Throwing us into a dilemma

Insisting us to losing stamina
Shaken is our self-confidence

This doubt hinders our achievements
Have not any doubt about yourself
Engage not in the double sword

Be clear in your thoughts
In doubt, you can't grow
Get out of this cobweb
Go ahead and never give up
Encourage yourself to believe in you
Select and decide what is good for you

The doubt will only let you go down

Engulfing all capabilities you own
No relations, no bonding is left
Engaging ourselves in this cobweb
Mundane will become the life
You will not be able to happily survive

11. HARD WORK SURELY PAYS OFF

Hey dear, work hard and never give up
After all, life is a test
Remember, you are capable of many things
Do not get disappointed if today you get nothing

Work enthusiastically till the end
O' you will surely get the fruit ripened
Result may be delayed
Keep up, you will be paid

Spider knits its web falling again and again
Under scorching sun a farmer ploughs his grains
Rider works hard to prepare for such a daunting act
Every student has to work hard to pass the test
Leaving the efforts gives you nothing
Yes, hard work will surely leads to blessings

Put all your efforts fully
Act always wisely

Yes, that day will not be far away
Success will enclose your pathway

O' then you will proudly say
Fruit of my efforts has ripened today
Father said truly, hard work pays

12. WEARING THE WINGS OF FANTASY

What an awesome feeling it is
Embracing the world of fantasy
Away from hustle and bustle of life
Relishing joyful dreams and desires
Igniting the fire in the water
Nostalgic moments with nature
Going above and holding the moon so tight

Touching peaks of mountains at a height
Humming and dancing like butterflies
Entering the world full of surprises

Wearing the wings of fantasy
***Imagine** being a galaxy*
Nuclear atoms, electrons, and photons
Glittering like silver and diamonds
Sometimes becoming a prince or princess

O' drowned in the nectar of love
Flying like a bird freely

Flowing like the water silently
Acting like an actor or actress
Number of emotions to express
That life would be so wonderful
Amazed, funny, and blissful
Sleeping in the lap of dreamland
Yodelling, singing, and doing romance

13. RELEASE YOURSELF FROM THE GUILT

Rivers and oceans look so beautiful
Embracing creatures that are dreadful
Life is the same way O' dear
Experiencing so many pains and fears
At times, we make some mistakes
Silly they are but become great
Engulfing us from inside

Yet, we keep them aside
O' but a moment comes in our life
Unpleasant becomes the way to survive
Relentless reminder of those mistakes
Somber our nights and days
Embarrassed we feel
Losing all potential and zeal
Floating in the ocean of repentance

Falling into the world of arrogance
Rendering us to move on
O' we always cry and mourn

Mundane become the world around

Tears flow with screaming sound
Having that guilt can we live ?
Extinguish the fire of that guilt

Good to remember that 'to err is human.
Under any guilt don't repent
Instead, look at its other side
Learn from it and move ahead in life
The guilt is a poison that kills from inside

14. THE WORLD IS A PLAY STAGE

The world is a play stage to play
Humans are actors playing in a unique way
Everyone plays their own role till the end

When the play ends, the curtain is turned
O' we are just puppets of divine hands
Role of everyone he only decides and plans
Laughing and smiling sometimes we cheer
Drowned in grief, we shed tears

Inspiring sometimes with our courageous acts
Sometimes get failed in life's tests

As a child, cherishing nostalgia for innocence
Playing and enjoying at the stage of adolescence
Love blooms into the young golden stage
Anxiety and pains in the old wrinkled age
Years pass away and the bell is rung

Story is about to reach an end
The role is over and the play is finished
And death knocks at life's field
Gone away we are, yet the role is remembered
Entertained by the whole world

15. EVEN THE DARKNESS HAS A LIGHT

Even if the night is too dark
Veil of this dark beholds a shimmering spark
Even if the monsoon clouds are black
New rays of rainbow dance in their lap

The same way, phases of life may be dark
Hopeless may become the life's path
Everywhere there may be a gloom of despair

Don't worry, still, light is there
A new door exists beyond the darkness
Reopening new ways toward brightness
Keep flowing on this life's pathway
New avenues you will cherish one day
Even if you fail again and again
Stop not and rebegin
Seek for light amidst the gloom

Hope for the best even in the doom

Aha! beautiful pictures are also developed in the dark
Same way, the gloom of life leaves a spark

After dark night, a bright morning arrives

Light of which induces positive vibes
In the same way, behind every gloom
Garden of abundant blessings bloom
Have not afraid of the word 'darkness'
The darkness is a path toward brightness

16. DO NOT ATTEMPT TO JUDGE OTHERS

Don't judge others so fast
O' don't unnecessarily ask

Never make any thinking for others
One does not know they are in which sphere
They may not respond as you expect

At times, they may play tact
They may act awkwardly
They seem to be unfriendly
Evaluate not their nature
Many of them do not behave in real
Pay gratitude for their gestures and offerings
Try to ignore other things

Tell them, they are wonderful
O' tell them, they are soulful

Just on the basis of a few actions
Unfair is to judge someone
Dancing and swinging don't mean always
Glittering in their way
Even behind their smile

Often they go through many odds and strides
The behavior that is shown outside
Helps not always to decide
Encourage them for their goodness
Respect them for what they possess
Surely, you will know the real facts

17. ALWAYS BE TRUE TO YOURSELF

Amazing and enigmatic is this life
Leads you toward a confusing side
Where you get caught in its cobweb
And you may even be ready to cheat yourself
Yet always remember one thing O' man
Stick to your principles in every situation

Be true to yourself as crystal clear
Everything will be fine, nothing to fear

The world may think anything about you
Remain always who are you
Under any circumstance, don't cheat yourself
Even if you find the time tough

Talk to your heart deep inside
O' no need to be fake from outside

You are a divine pious soul
O' you must know about yourself as a whole
Ushering desires will mislead you
Remember, you have to be always true
Stay committed to your inner self
Enlighten within a truthful candle for yourself
Live each moment remembering your conscious
Forget the world, but donot forget yourself

18. BE KIND AND COMPASSIONATE

Be kind and dwell in empathy
Enlighten a candle of peace and harmony

Keep a heart enlivened with generosity
Indulge within the virtues of humanity
Never ever hurt anyone in any way
Do something soulful each and every day

Always listen to others' pain and worries
No matter, how much you have miseries
Deeds of compassion bring smiles to abound

Come out of your comfort and look around
O' wipe off others' painful tears
Make someone's life bloom like flowers
Put your efforts to help others selflessly
Always lend your shoulder to the needy
Sow a seed of kindness and humanity
Spread all around a divine serenity

Inspire others with your kind gestures
O' human life is a blessing to us
Never ruin your life by making it fuss
Always keep alive your heartiness
Take a moment to eradicate others' tensions
Enrich their life with mirth and passion

19. DO BELIEVE IN YOUR DREAMS

Dreams are the guides of our life
O' even awaken keep them alive

Believe in your dreams O' dear
Enliven them forever and cheer
Let these dreams be your inspiration
Ignite within a flicker of determination
Even if your dreams do not come true
Victory may not always embrace you
Even if everything seems to be unfair

In no way stop dreaming O' dear
Never be afraid of chasing your dreams and passion

Yes, it takes some time for everything to happen
On the way, there may be odd situations
Unfortunate may be your destiny even
Roses may not bloom always your way

Dear, but never stop dreaming even when awake
Road may be far away from what you have chosen
Every day is passed; every night may be gone
Again, smile and cherish your dreams fully
Mysterious are these dreams and their story
Surely, one day they come true gifting you with glory

20. PEACE COMES FROM WITHIN

Peace is a divine blessing to us
Enriches life with eternal mirth
Awakening soul and spirit within
Creating a temple so pious and serene
Enlightening a candle of divinity

Connecting pathway to Almighty
O' peace comes from within my dear
Mold your inner self and cheer
Eradicate all envy and violence
Stay always calm and silent

Forget everything, forgive all
Remain peaceful even if you fall
O' you can move to China or Greece
Most blissful place is our inner peace

Welcome divine thoughts in mind
Ignite the flicker of peace so divine

Thank God for every blessing
Have a smile even in the suffering
In the real sense, peace exists inside
Not in the myth world outside

21. BE GRATEFUL FOR EVERYTHING

Blessed you are to get this life
Endless treasures it always provides

God has given you the birth of a human
Regard him for whatever he has given
Always be grateful for your blessings
Thank Lord for each and everything
Even be grateful for the sufferings
For these teach you valuable teachings
Unfold the curtain of life
Look, so many bountiful gifts it hides

For breath blowing, heart beating
O' for the blood flowing, body working
Regard that you awake each morning

Even amidst disguise, you have blessings
Vast is the list of these treasures
Every moment pays gratitude and cheer

Rarely we all gets this life
Yet we ruin it for our fake pride
There are some faces that can't smile even
Having no joy and fun
In your hands, there are so many blessings
Nourish them by thankful sayings
Gratefulness will itself dwell in your surroundings

22. DARE TO REACH FOR THE STARS

Dear, this life is a blessing
Aspire to achieve something
Rock on even amidst the odds
Engage your mind in daring thoughts

The sky can be in your hands
O' dare to bring the stars on the land

Road of life is very tough
Every path has an untoward twist
Anyways, dare to cross that road
Cross even the limits of the world
Have a goal to touch even the sky

Flying freely above so high
O' dare to reach for the stars
Remember your destination is so far

Take the charge of your own life
Have the courage to win every strife
Enthusiastically put all efforts

Surely you will get your results
Take a flight of determination
And you will accomplish your mission
Raise like a Phoenix and move on
Stars are waiting, dare to reach on

23. MEMORABLE MOMENTS OF TIME

Moments of time are very special
Every moment is unforgettable
Maybe it is too short to live
Or it may be too long to greet
Running with time, moments pass
Add up new moments for last
Beautiful is the perception of these moments
Letting us cherish our time spent
Entwined altogether

Make memories forever
O' sometimes end in silent screams
Much pains, tears, and unfulfilled dreams
Enveloping the pages of life's diary
Number of unforgettable memories
Tuning and dancing in sweet melody
Sometimes dull, dry and empty

O' amazing are these moments
Float freely in the ocean of dreamland

The moments never stop, they move on
In every moment something is hidden
Memories become unforgettable lessons
Enriching life with experiences to learn

24. REAL JOY OF GIVING OTHERS

Rare treasure is this human life
Enriching us with so many virtues inside
And these virtues are a reflection of the great Almighty
Letting us live joyfully

Journey of life is amazing
O' there is a special joy in giving
You always do for your own needs

O' real joy is to do for others indeed
Forgetting own pains bringing smiles to others

Giving helping hands to some helpless
In the barren lives filling colors
Venturing like a fighter for others
In empty eyes, painting dreams of passion
Nothing is more joyful than dwelling on compassion
Generously giving with an open heart

O' joy is to spread harmony in every part
Taking away others' miseries
Hey, joy is to resolve their worries
Eternal mirth is cherished with this joyful act
Respectful we become for the life in fact
Smile itself comes with these joyful tacts

25. THE PATH THAT WE CHOOSE

The pathways of life is not so easy
Hurdles may enclose its vivid phases
Explore it deeply before you move

Path may be tough that we choose
At every step there may be untoward challenges
There may be worst circumstances
Hopeless may be the situations

This depends on us, how do we reach our destination
Having courage and determination
Alas! losing our enthusiasm
There is no end, we find this way

Wisely we have to follow our way
Embracing its troughs and crests

Climbing slowly slowly doing our the best
Having self-belief and faith
O' we have to chase life's race
Obviously, there is not always a bed of rose
Steps taken decide where do your life goes
Every path you have to carefully explore

26. LOVE IS THE LIGHT IN MURK

Love is a wonderful blessing of the Lord
O' with its euphoria it eradicates all hatred
Vibrating melodious musings
Enriches life in lifeless living

Igniting a candle of divinity
Sowing a seed of ecstasy

Turning all disguises into blessings
Healing every wound and suffering
Energizing a hope to live again

Love is a balm for every pain
It blooms bare land into a garden
Gifts life with bundles of passions
Hues and shades of lovable colors
Turn life's pages into a beautiful canvas

It is not only a word but the breath of life
Not visible, not held, yet alive

Magnificent treasure that we earn
Under its embrace, every place is heaven
Ray of light in the murk
Kaleidoscope of feelings is this 'love'

27. LET GO OFF THE THINGS

Life is a blessing, we get it only once
Every moment is a new chance and new experience
Then why to waste it in arguments

Grudges, hatered and violence
O' learn to let go off the things

O' all of us are human beings
For the silly mistakes we forgive ourselves
For fake pride we love ourselves

Then why to punish someone else for little mistakes
Hey why to dwell anger and hate
Erase all discrepencies and complaints

Take things lightly without feeling pains
Have courage to let go off and move on
It is silly to carry grudges and linger on

Nobody knows when this life will end
Greatness is to forget and not offend
Same life you will never get hey friend

28. PRAYER HAS A MIRACULOUS POWER

Pray every moment O' dear
Recognize its miraculous power
Amazing is that moment
Yielding results are so pleasant
Enlightening a candle of divinity
Rewarding us with eternal ecstasy

Healing from all sufferings
Awakening us from within
Spreading a ray of new hope and peace

Angles of Lord silently tweet

Meditating with the divine energy
Ignite a flicker of empathy
Relieving all negative vibes
Amen, we say, in a confident voice
Confessing all fears and pains in front of the Lord
Under his grace, we find abundant love

Love that heals all our wounds
O' we can see light even in the gloom
Unbelievable is the magic of prayer
Silently it makes us so light and cheer

Praying and bowing in the court of God
O' sends a message to the whole world
Whole word is cherished like a divine temple
Even the impossible turns into possible
Really, the prayer brings a miracle

29. BE AN INSPIRATION FOR OTHERS

Be a person who can inspire others
Eradicating all worries and fears

Act boldly at every step of life
Never ever get tired of strife

Illuminate within the flicker of enthusiasm
Never ever lose self-determination
Stay optimistic even in an odd phase
Put your efforts till the last stage
Inspire others through your hard work and struggle
Remember you can always bring miracles
A word of courage, love, and motivation is enough
That can encourage others even when everything seems tough
In this world, you have a unique identity
O' you never know when you become an inspiration for somebody
Never forget that you can scribble a golden history

For others, you can bring a change positively

O' even after you die, you remain an example
Recognizing your strength can bring miracles

Others must follow in your footsteps
They should learn your tacts
Have such an honor in your hands
Everyone yearns to know your plans
Rendering them to move further
Set an inspirational role for others

30. MUSIC HEALS EVERY PAIN

Music seems to be a small word
Unbelievable are its effects
Seven swars and their melody
Influental for everybody
Can bring smiles all around

Heal someone's unhealed wound
Enlighten a candle of peace
Awakening inner consience
Leaving a magical spell
Suddenly bring miracles

Enchanting lyrics and rhythms
Vivid forms of divine rhymes
Enrich life with profound joy and mirth
Repair even the scars left
Yoddeling and dancing drowned in these rhythms

Pain goes away all of sudden
Aha! music beholds some magical stick
In bare life, colours it fills
Nature's bountiful blessing is music

31. RIGHT TIME WILL COME SOON

Remember dear, sometimes life becomes unfair
In every moment you dwell in despair
Gone days were full of pains
Hoping for a smile might have gone in vain
There is always a hope yet

This life sometimes takes a test
It is not that this life remains rough always
Moments of joy also come one day
Efforts made by you may get failed

Wait, but there is a right time always
In the long wait, there must be something hidden
Life will disclose it in the long turn
Leave all hopelessness aside

Come on, have patience and smile
O' nothing is permanent you know this fact
Make sure you put in your efforts

Eradicate all pains and worries

Soon you will cherish life's beauty
O' don't get drowned in the ocean of gloom
O' don't make your life a hopeless doom
No worries, the right time will come soon

32. OUR HEART IS A BEAUTIFUL GARDEN

O' deep inside this body there is a beautiful place
Under its embrace, we cherish Lord's divine grace
Rare treasure it is for everyone

Heart is nothing but a beautiful garden
Every seed of feelings and emotions is sowed here
And that bloom into its flowers
Rejuvenate this garden with the seeds of humanity
That can grow into a tree of prosperity

Indulge this garden with nutrients of love
Seal the roots with caring mud

Always take care of its growth

Bury all garbage that it beholds
Enrich this garden with the aroma of divinity
Add a composite of love and empathy

Under any situation, don't ruin its existence
Throw away all seeds of envy and arrogance
Flowers of this garden are unique and special
Unconditionally embrace every particle
Let this garden be blooming forever

Grow in it trees of joy and laughter
Abode of divine power is this garden
Relished like a blissful heaven
Dare not to spoil its presence
Enrich it with lovable nutrients
Never ever let it be barren

33. BE THE LEADER OF YOUR LIFE

Be the leader of your life
Explore new avenues even amidst odds and strifes

Take the charge in your hands
Have focused goals and plans
Erase the thought 'what others say

Lead your life in your own way
Energize your mind with positive thoughts
Adore the life that you behold
Dauntlessly take on every step.
Enthusiastically work and never give up.
Respect others' views, but don't follow.

O' do whatever you feel so.
Face every hurdle alone.

You will win the successful crown.
O' your path may be tough.
Until you die, don't stop.
Recognize your inner potential.

Let impossible be turned into possible.
In no way, let others lead you.
Follow your path, chosen by you.
Embrace the life framed by you.

34. KNOCK THE BLISSFUL DOOR

Knock the blissful door
New things you must explore
O' it is a door that welcomes a new world
Cumulated with virtues of divine love
Keep the pains of the past aside

Take a new flight
Hold the keys to this door in your hands
Encourage yourself to make new plans

Blissful life is waiting for you
Love and mirth are made for you
In this new world cherish a fresh life.
Slowly - slowly step inside
Stay peacefully with eternal bliss
Forget about all that you missed
Uncountable are the blessings here
Leashing this door will leave you bare

Do *not worry about anything*
O' a new world is waiting
Optimistically *be ready to hold precious pearls*
Relish life's amazing miracles

35. WE DO NOT GET MATCHES ALWAYS

We all are known as humans
Even then we are different

Different thoughts, different thinking
*Our life **is** different, different is the living*

Not always do we get the matches
O' all have different tastes
The destination is different

Goals are different
Everyone has got own perceptions
Their own assumptions

Mind acts differently
All of us are having own identities
This is not possible to get the same matches
Compatibility sometimes mismatches

Have not many expectations from others
Every time don't expect the same features
Stop having high expectations

Admire each and every creation
Let go of the things
Which don't create matching
Accept others as they are
You are you, unique you are
So, learn to love, admire and cheer

36. NOTHING IS IMPOSSIBLE FOR YOU

Nothing is impossible here
Optimistically move on in life's every sphere
Tough may be the pathway
Hurdles may enclose your ways
In many aspects, you may fail and break down
Not always do you hold the successful crowns
Getting failed you are hurt

In this world, you feel nothing is worth
Still, never give up O' dear

In spite of all this, face everything without any fear
Move on with inner zeal and enthusiasm
Pick up the weapons of courage and determination
O' keep igniting the flicker of self-inspiration
Stay strong and focused to achieve your ambition
Surely you will cherish amazing miracles
Impossible will get turned into possible
Blessed you are to get this wonderful life
Life may be tough, but you can cross every stride

End will be fruitful, have patience

Fear not to reattempt
O' courageous are those, who stay strong
Raise again even being alone

You have the power, you can do anything
O' never give up, keep on moving
Until you achieve your desired thing

37. KEEP ALIVE YOUR PAIN WITHIN

Keep alive your pain within
Embrace it without fearing anything
Extinguishing its fire extinguishes your strength
Pain is a scar that reminds you about your wound

Awakens you to fight again
Lesson to learn becomes your pain
Igniting inner enthusiasm
Vanishing all bareness within
Energizing your inner power

Your pain makes you a warrior
O' it reminds you about your mistakes
Unnecessarily on many, you kept the faith
Reimplanting seeds of courage and determination

Pain is a guide to leading your mission
Although it dwells an ocean of tears within
In spite of this, it takes us to joyful heaven

Never forget, your biggest strength becomes your pain

When you have to face some new situation
It reminds you to take caution
Taking you back toward your mistakes
Helping you in the decisions you take
In one way, pain is your best dude
Nurturing your self-confidence and attitude

38. ALWAYS LISTEN TO YOUR HEART

Appreciate what others say or advice
Lend your ear to listen to their choice
Walking on life's pathway
All of us meet many people in different ways
Yes, no doubt, sometimes they may be right
Sometimes valuable is their advice

Listen to them, but not always follow
It is you who has to decide where to go
Sit silently with your closed eyes
Talk to your heart and its voice
Enlighten your inner awakening
Note, whatever your heart is saying

Take the charge of your own life
O' look, deep inside

You will listen to a voice at that moment
O' that will lead you to take the action

Understand the message hidden in that
Reciprocate it by saying "YES"

Have faith in your heart inside
Everything it will tell the right
Always do passionate things carefree
Read what is written in the heart's diary
Throw away all your worry

39. TAKE A MOMENT TO REFLECT

Time passes away
And memorable becomes each day
Kaleidoscope of those memories is imprinted within the heart
Enriching our life with joy until death departs

Aha! take a moment to reflect

Make your memories afresh
O' go into the world of your childhood
Moments you had cherished with dudes
Enlighten a candle of innocence within
Nostalgic moments will be cherished again
Endless are those moments
Take a look without missing any chance

Turn out the pages of your life's book
O' it was amazing, just have a look

Refresh your memories and cherish their presence
Eradicate all grudges and arrogance
Fill your life with colours of those moments
Let go of stress and enjoy your present
Enrich your mind with cheerful memories
Cut off all unnecessary worries
Take a moment to reflect O' buddy

40. ASPIRATION IS LIKE A FLYING BIRD

As a bird flies high in the sky

Spreading the wings with a smile
Preparing every day to reach the destination
In the same way, is 'aspiration'
Ready to fly every day
Aspiring for a new way
There are no limits to fly
It wants to reach even beyond the sky
O' it spreads its wings so vast
No worries about what others are going to talk

It has its own world
Same way as the bird

Longing to embrace even unbelievable things
In the sky of dreamland, it spreads its wings
Knitting its nest with sticks of effort
Enthusiastically it accomplishes its work

Aware both are, that someone is ready to break their wings

Fear is there, but they fear nothing
Leaving all worries both keep on flying
Yearn to attain what they are aspiring
In a silent melody, they cheer the surroundings
Nurturing the heart with abundant blessings
Giving spirit to do something

Begin again even if failing
Ignite the flicker of determination within
Road is tough, but both aspire to win
Dauntlessly, both spread their wings

41. EVRYONE HAS EQUAL RIGHT TO LIVE

Each of us is God's creation
Vivid shades, languages, and religions
Even then we all are human
Races may differ, and rituals may be different
Yet, we all are known as humans
O' every one of us has an equal right to live
No one can do any injustice
Everyone has their own way and choice

Having own ideas and style
All of us live in the same world
Same sky, and same earth

Every one of us are the same Lord's children
Question is then why there is discrimination?
Unfortunately why are people treated unequally here ?
Alas! just on the base of color?
Let there be justice all around

Remove discrimination and bury injustice in the ground
In the faux pas of this discrimination
Genuine deservers lag behind
Hoping to achieve their ambitions
To live their life with love and passion

Though we belong to an independent world
O' but yet there is no freedom dwell

Let us all live and let others live
Indulging humanity and justice
Vanishing discrimination forever
Enrich everyone's life with joy and cheer

42. EVEN THE RICHEST IS THE POOREST

Everyone says, O' he is the richest
Variety of comforts he has
Everyone says loudly
None can be as rich as he is

The truth is not always what we see
Having everything even sometimes we always plead
Enriched are those who are living peacefully

Relishing their life joyfully
Everything is there; money, comfort
Alas! Still, there is always a distress
Canopy of inner pains inside
Heaving heavily with silent cries
Every moment there is a stress
Sailing in the ocean of richness
They are still the poorest

In search of love and mirth
Sometimes, they lack a rich heart

That does not know to impart
Having abundant money
Even they can't donate a single penny

Poor they are who don't have heartiness
O' who are not generous
***Obtaining** money and luxury don't mean everything*
Real richness is being rich in giving
Even being richest drowned in the gloom of despair
Such a kind of life is unfair
There may be richness, but then also life is poor

43. WE ALL ARE DANCERS, BUT WE FORGET

We are blessed with a wonderful life
Enriching us with its silent smile
Alas! we fail to admire its rhythmic flow
Lost in our agony and ego
Lively music plays in its lap

And we forget to dance and clap
Reality is that every one of us knows this fact
Expert we are, we all are dancers to rock on life's tract

Dancing does not need any perfectness
Accepting everything joyfully dwells on this act
No rules, no restrictions, no limits
Chasing down lovable heartbeats
Enchanting songs on rhymes of life
Rolling and dancing like a child
Sad is the fact that we keep on mourning

Blessed we are, yet keep on cursing
Unlock the key to happiness O' dear
Take little steps, dance, and cheer

When you look at life's real side
Enthusiastically you will love its vibes

Forgetting every pain and worry
O' dance and sing joyfully
Relish whatever life brings to you
Great boon it will be proved for you
Enriching your world with profound mirth
Then you will feel blissful to get this birth

44. SOLVE, BUT DO NOT CARRY ON

Sometimes we have misunderstandings
O' we discuss and solve everything
Lest sometimes we carry on the past
Very difficult it is for us to re-start
Engaged in our thoughts we knit a cobweb

Begin to get caught in it on ourselves
Ushering thoughts complicates our matter
Taking us back again rather
Dear, good is to solve and move on further
O' do not get caught in this web anymore
Nothing you will gain
O' rather only pain
Taking you away from your inner peace

Crumbled you will with your solace
Aha! Life is too short, we get it only once
Remove all grudges and arrogance
Restart the things and forget
You will feel comfortable and blessed

O' remember, solve but not carry on
Not allow your life to become doom

45. CRY BUT ONLY IN YOUR EMBRACE

Crying is not bad O' dear
Release your pain and flow tears
Yes, remember one thing always

But cry only in your embrace
Unexpected are the people
They do not always understand your tears

O' rather in this busy world
None has got time for others
Lost in own matters
Your pain they least bother

It is much better to cry all alone
Nobody is always staying along

You can express every emotion to yourselves
O' shed of all fears and guilts

Under your own embrace
Rejoice you own tears

Expressing here, nobody will ignore
Many more experiences you can explore
Bonding with your inner self becomes stronger
Really, you feel much better
Alas! The world just watches and laughs
Can't feel the depth of every talk
Express your pain only to your heart

46. LOVE YOURSELF FIRST TO LOVE OTHERS

Love is not just a word
O' a deep meaning it disperses
Very often, we love others
Engaged in them, we forget ourselves

You are unique, you are lovable
O' first learn to love yourself
Unleash the lock of happiness
Respect your inner self
Start loving your essence
Embrace your own fragrance
Lit a candle of love inside
Fall in love with you from every side

First, learn to respect your own priorities
Indulge within your responsibility
Remember, none can love you as much as your own
So many will claim, but none
To love someone else

The self-love you have to dwell
O' if you care for yourself

Love yourself
Obviously then only
Very truly you will love others
Enrich their life's garden with lovable flowers

O' but you ignore yourself
Trying to impress someone else
Have a seed of love sown in your heart
Embrace love in each and every part
Real treasure you will earn
Surrounded by love and passion

47. BEHOLD THE HEART OF A CHILD FOREVER

Blessed you are to get this blissful life
Elated to get a beautiful heart inside
Hovering in the sky of life
O' we forget, how to joyfully survive
Live your life like a child
Dwell innocence inside

Throw away all garbage of sins
Happily cherish everything
Even if you get old

Heart of a child you always behold
Enriched with pure thoughts
Aha! A reflection of the divine Lord
Reciprocate others with your harmless smile
Throw magic with your cute style

O' even amidst the hustle and bustle of life
Forever live as if you are a child

Aspire for your passionate things

Capture butterflies dancing and humming
Hate not for anything around
In every phase keep smiling with miles of smiles abound
Let old wrinkled skin be smiling forever
Do whatever you want to do O' dear

Forgetting about the whole world
Only cherish your own love
Recall the moments of your childhood
Enliven them forever even in solitude
Vigorous may become life's path
Even then you do not lose your heart
Relish joyfully life's each and every part

48. UNIVERSE IS AN ETHEREAL MEDIUM

Universe; a wonderful creation
Nobody knows where it ends, from where it begins
It is an ethereal medium
Vibrate in its ears without beating any drum
Entwine your ushering thoughts
Release in the lap of the universe
Speak clearly whatever you wish to attain
Energize it with your positive brain

It will listen to your every word
Sending your message to the world

And the divine powers start showing their actions
New ways and doors they open

Entering those doors your thoughts get revived
Turning back to you with positive vibes
Holding your hands to open them widely
Entangling abundant love and prosperity

Rewarding you with all your ambitions
Encouraging you to fulfill your missions
And you will see that magic happens
Leading your life toward a new direction

Molding you thinking in a different way
Enriched become your every day
Dear, the universe beholds a magical wand
In its embrace, you can achieve blessings in your hands
Unsaid words, silently speaking
Miraculous moments you will start cherishing

49. STAY FOCUSED TO ACHIEVE YOUR AIM

Setting goals is very easy
To accomplish them may be uneasy
A direction is needed to move on
You have to properly work on

Focus on the goal that you set
On that then you act
Concentrating solely on that
Unimportant must be the things left
Set it as your utmost priority
Engage yourself in it fully
Deviate not from your focus

Think not about others
O' without focus nothing is possible

And once focused, you can achieve even the impossible
Chose your path and direction
Help yourself to achieve your mission

Ignite a flicker of enthusiasm
Energetically move on.
Victory you will attain one day
Everything you will find on your way

You recall the stories of history
O' how winners attained their glory
Unique was their way of accomplishment
Relying on just their mission

And leaving everything else aside
In their mind, only their aim resides
Moving in the right direction, they attained whatever desired

50. SMILE IS THE BIGGEST ASSET

Smile, smile, keep on smiling
Make your life a wonderful blessing
It is the curve that keeps life straight
Live every moment with a smile, why wait
Enrich your surroundings with your innocent smile

It is a magical wand to cross every stride
Smile is a virtue that can touch millions of hearts

Through its spark, it can illuminate even the dark
Hiding your own tears keep on smiling
Even if everything is unfair, leave worrying

Bountiful treasures are hidden in this smile
In its embrace, you can cross miles
Glow like a diamond beholding this smile
Greet the world with your jolly style
Even if you get enclosed by the gloom of despair
Smile will leave a shimmering spark there

ACROSTIC MOTIVATIONS

The world may leave you all alone

Aha! your smile will always make you strong
So, what for you are waiting
Smile is the biggest asset and blessing
Enlighten a candle of smile within
Throw away all worries in the bin